Bear Hugs for Meals and Snacks

Positive activities for calm, enjoyable meals and snacks

By Patty Claycomb

Illustrated by Marion Hopping Ekberg

TOTLINE BOOKS

Warren Publishing House, Inc.
Everett, Washington

Editorial Staff
  Editorial Manager: Kathleen Cubley
  Editor: Gayle Bittinger
  Contributing Editors: Susan Hodges, Elizabeth McKinnon,
    Jean Warren
  Copy Editor: Kris Fulsaas
  Proofreader: Mae Rhodes
  Editorial Assistants: Kate Ffolliott, Erica West

Design and Production Staff
  Art Managers: Uma Kukathas, Jill Lustig
  Book Design/Layout: Sarah Ness
  Cover Design/Layout: Brenda Mann Harrison
  Electronic Coloration: Mae Rhodes
  Cover Illustration: Marion Hopping Ekberg
  Bear Hugs Logo: Susan Dahlman
  Production Manager: Jo Anna Brock

Copyright © 1994 by Warren Publishing House, Inc. All rights reserved. Except for including brief quotations in a review, no part of this book may be reproduced in any form without the written consent of the publisher.

ISBN 1-57029-015-6

Printed in the United States of America
Published by: Warren Publishing House, Inc.
        P.O. Box 2250
        Everett, WA 98203

20 19 18 17 16 15 14 13 12 11 10 9 8 7 6 5 4 3 2 1

Introduction

Meals and snacks are some of the most fascinating times of the day for your children. Socialization is at its best. You can observe your children talking, laughing, giggling, whispering, teasing, bragging, comparing, questioning, planning, and, yes, even eating.

All of this wonderful socialization encourages not only fun and friendship, but noise. Noise can be a happy, active sound, but at meals or snacks, it can easily distract from eating and become "too much." When this happens, just pull out one of the simple Bear Hug activities in this book. These activities are designed to help your children keep their noise level down and remember their table manners.

Like the other books in the Bear Hugs series, *Bear Hugs for Meals and Snacks* provides you with positive approaches to preventing potential problems. Noise will no longer be an issue as you use the ideas in this book to help your children eat and socialize in a calm and relaxed atmosphere.

Contents

Noisy-Quiet Rhyme 6

The Hungry Rhyme 7

Cookout 8

Night Animal 9

Lightning Flash 10

Mouse, Mouse, Come Out 11

Peanut Drop 12

Traffic Signal 13

Musical Meals 14

Lunch-Pail Stickers 15

The Promise Tree 16

Placemat Game 17

Airplane Ride 18

Snowball Fun 19

Surprise Egg 20

The Magic Bird 21

Noisy-Quiet Rhyme

Try this Bear Hug to encourage your children to begin eating in a calm and happy manner.

Materials: None.

Preparation: None.

Activity: Have your children sit down with their meal or snack. Tell them that you are going to say a noisy and quiet rhyme with them. Then lead them in the first verse below, acting out the motions and using normal voices.

> **I can roar like a dinosaur.**
> *(Roar.)*
> **I can stomp my feet.**
> *(Stomp feet.)*
> **I can clap my hands,**
> *(Clap hands.)*
> **I can sit in my seat.**
> *(Sit very still in chair.)*

Tell the children that this was the noisy part of the rhyme. Have them lower their voices while they say the final quiet verse.

> **I can roar in a whisper,**
> *(Roar very quietly.)*
> **I can tap my feet.**
> *(Tap feet.)*
> **I can twiddle my fingers,**
> *(Wiggle fingers.)*
> **Now I'm ready to eat.**
> *(Place hands in lap.)*

Extension: Have your children make up their own Noisy-Quiet Rhyme. Ask them to suggest four noisy actions and three quiet actions. Always end the rhyme with "Now I'm ready to eat." (Don't worry about words that rhyme. Results are what count.)

The Hungry Rhyme

*Use this Bear Hug to help your children settle down
and get ready to eat.*

Materials: None.

Preparation: None.

Activity: After your children are seated at the tables, say the following rhyme. Let them act out the motions with you.

>I am hungry and I want to eat,
>>(Rub tummy.)
>
>But am I ready for my treat?
>
>First I'm going to check my feet—
>>(Point to feet.)
>
>Two quiet mice, under my seat.
>>(Put feet under chair.)
>
>Now for my hands, they're quiet too,
>>(Hold up hands.)
>
>Just like the crocodiles in the zoo.
>>(Place hands on table.)
>
>There's a small buzz coming out of me,
>>(Buzz quietly.)
>
>My voice is as quiet as a bumblebee.
>>(Hold finger to lips.)
>
>Now I'm ready, as you can see,
>>(Sit up straight in chair.)
>
>And hungry—as a bear can be!
>>(Rub tummy.)

Now let the children eat their snack or meal. If they need a reminder, ask them questions such as these: "What should your feet be like? Are your hands quiet like crocodiles? Do you sound like bumblebees?"

7

Cookout

Use this Bear Hug to spark your children's imaginations while helping them remember to be quiet.

Materials: Aluminum foil; toothpicks.

Preparation: Tear off a piece of aluminum foil for each child.

Activity: Explain to your children that they will be camping and having a Cookout while they eat today. Dim the lights and pull down the shades to make it look like nighttime. Tell the children that they need to be quiet when they are camping so they won't scare away the animals. Encourage the children to talk in low voices about the animals they might see.

Serve the children their meal or snack. Then tell them that it is time for the Cookout. Pass out the pieces of aluminum foil. Let the children wrap the foil around pieces of food from their meal or snack. Give each child a few toothpicks to arrange in a pile to create a "fire." Let the children pretend to cook their foil-wrapped foods over their fires. When their food is "roasted," it is time to eat.

Variations: Give your children mini-marshmallows stuck on the ends of toothpicks. Let them "roast" their marshmallows over their toothpick fires. To add to the feeling of being outdoors, play recorded sounds of rain, a running stream, or wild animals.

Night Animal

Encourage your children to be more calm and quiet with this Bear Hug.

Materials: A toy animal that represents a nocturnal animal such as an owl, a bat, a firefly, a hamster, or a coyote.

Preparation: None.

Activity: Place the toy animal near the place where your children eat. Explain to the children that this special animal has joined them for their meal or snack. Tell them that the animal is nocturnal, which means it likes a dark and quiet room best. Then turn off the lights.

Tell the children that the Night Animal will stay with them as long as the room stays quiet and dark. If the noise level gets too high, turn on the lights and remind the children that the Night Animal will have to leave if it is too noisy. Turn off the lights as the noise subsides.

If the Night Animal has remained throughout the entire meal or snack, let the children pet it as they leave for their next activity.

Variation: Let your children save small parts of their food (a raisin, a bite of crust, a piece of cracker, etc.) to "feed" the Night Animal.

Hint: Keep the Night Animal stored away and have it visit only at meals or snacks.

Lightning Flash

Use this Bear Hug to foster quiet at meals or snacks.

Materials: Flashlight.

Preparation: None.

Activity: Dim the lights in your room. Tell your children that a thunderstorm is coming. Switch the flashlight on and off to show them the "lightning" from the storm. Then say the rhyme below, inserting *lunch* or *snack* in the blank as appropriate.

> **Lightning, lightning**
> **In the sky,**
> **Painting pictures**
> **Way up high.**
>
> **Lighting up**
> **The kids below,**
> **Eating their _____**
> **Quiet and slow.**

Give the flashlight to a child who is eating quietly. Let the child shine the flashlight and turn it off and on while you say the last verse of the rhyme, inserting the child's name in the blank.

> **Now it's _____'s turn**
> **To take the light,**
> **And make strange pictures**
> **In the night.**

Repeat the rhyme from the beginning, allowing the child with the flashlight to give it to another child who is eating quietly. Make sure each quiet child has a chance to hold the flashlight.

Mouse, Mouse, Come Out

Use this Bear Hug to help your children remember to keep the noise level down.

Materials: Small toy mouse; string; shoe box; scissors.

Preparation: Tie a piece of string around the mouse. Make a mouse house by cutting a hole big enough for the mouse to fit through on one side of the shoe box. Place the mouse in the house with its string hanging out of the hole.

Activity: Place the mouse house near the tables where your children eat. When the children sit down to eat, explain that in this house there lives a mouse who is very afraid of noise. If the mouse hears too much noise, it will not come out.

When the children are eating and socializing in a calm manner, ask the mouse to come out by having everyone say quietly, "Mouse, Mouse, come out." Select a child to pull on the string to make the mouse come out. Let the mouse sit on the table with the children. Remind them that if it gets too loud, the mouse will be afraid and jump back into its house.

Let the mouse sit at the table as long as it is quiet. If the noise level gets too high, put the mouse back in its house. Let another child pull it out again when the noise level goes back down.

At the end of the meal or snack, if the mouse is outside its house, let each child pet it as he or she leaves for the next activity.

Hint: Make a mouse and a mouse house for each table of children.

Peanut Drop

Encourage an appropriate noise level with this Bear Hug.

Materials: Small plastic jar; unshelled peanuts.

Preparation: None.

Activity: Place the jar where all your children can see it. Tell them that you will be listening for quiet noise and that when you hear it, you will put a peanut in the jar. If the jar is full at the end of the meal or snack, each child will get to select a peanut from the jar to shell and eat.

Variation: Instead of putting in the peanuts yourself, select quiet children to put the peanuts in the jar.

Traffic Signal

Use this Bear Hug to help your children recognize when their talking is becoming too loud.

Materials: White, red, yellow, and green construction paper; scissors; non-aluminum baking sheet; double-sided tape; magnets; glue.

Preparation: Cut three identical circles out of the white construction paper. Cut the same size circles out of the red, yellow, and green construction paper, one circle from each color. Arrange the red, yellow, and green circles on the baking sheet to make it look like a traffic signal. Fasten the circles in place with double-sided tape. Glue a magnet to the back of each white circle. Place the white circles over each circle on the baking sheet.

Activity: Show your children the Traffic Signal. Show the children just the green "light" by removing the white circle from the green one. Explain that when they see the green "light" it means that the noise level is just right. Show the children just the yellow light and tell them that it means the noise level is starting to get too high. Then show them just the red light. Explain that when they see this, they must stop talking until they see the green light again.

Then let the children eat their meal or snack. Monitor the noise level while they are eating and adjust the Traffic Signal as necessary.

Musical Meals

Help your children remember to use quiet voices at meals or snacks with this Bear Hug.

Materials: Music box with off and on switch.

Preparation: None.

Activity: Have your children sit down and begin their snacks or lunches. Wind up the music box and set it where all the children can watch and hear it. (Use more than one music box, if necessary.) Tell the children that when they are eating and visiting quietly, they will be able to hear the music box play. When the noise level gets too high, turn off the music box until everyone is quiet again. Turn on the music box when the noise is at an appropriate level again.

Variation: Instead of a music box, use a battery-operated lantern (available at sporting-goods stores). Tell your children that this is a magic lantern that will only stay lit when they are eating and visiting quietly.

Lunch-Pail Stickers

Use this Bear Hug to encourage your children to remember their table manners.

Materials: Construction paper; scissors; stapler; felt-tip marker; tape; stickers.

Preparation: Fold a piece of construction paper in half. Cut the top half as shown in the illustration to make a handle. Staple the paper together on both sides to make a "lunch pail." Make one for each child. Write a child's name on each lunch pail and tape it on a wall near the tables where the children eat.

Activity: Discuss table manners with your children. Let them pretend to eat while using manners and not using manners. Talk about why we want to use manners.

Then show the children the lunch pails. Help each child find the lunch pail with his or her name on it. Explain that each time you see one of the children using table manners, you will give that child a sticker to put on his or her pail. (Make sure to catch each child using table manners at least once each day.) At the end of the week, let the children take their sticker-covered lunch pails home.

15

The Promise Tree

Use this Bear Hug to remind your children to talk quietly and use their table manners.

Materials: Butcher paper; felt-tip markers; crayons; various colors of construction paper; scissors; tape.

Preparation: Draw a large tree trunk with many branches on the butcher paper. Draw a hole on the trunk. Let your children help color the tree. Hang the tree near the tables where the children eat. Cut leaf shapes out of construction paper. Tape the leaves to the branches of the tree. Write the name of a promised treat on a small strip of construction paper. (The treat could be a tent day, a puppet show, a special art project, etc.) Fold the paper with the promise written on it and tape it to the hole on the tree trunk.

Activity: Talk about the tree with your children. Tell them that it is a Promise Tree that will offer them a promise only when its branches are covered with leaves. Explain that the leaves stay on the branches when it is quiet and children are using their manners, but that too much noise or forgetting manners makes the leaves fall off.

Leave the Promise Tree up for a week. When the noise at meals or snacks becomes too much or the children are forgetting to use their manners, move a few of the leaves to the bottom of the tree. When a more appropriate noise level or the use of manners returns, put the leaves back on the branches.

At the end of the week, if the branches are covered with leaves, read the promise and then do whatever it says with the children.

Placemat Game

Encourage your children to use table manners and quiet voices with this Bear Hug.

Materials: Paper placemats; felt-tip marker; rubber stamps; ink pad.

Preparation: Write one of your children's names on each placemat. Set the placemats out on the tables where your children eat.

Activity: Have your children find their placemats and sit down in front of them. Explain to your children that when you see them using table manners or quiet voices, you will come by and stamp designs on their placemats. If necessary, review table manners and demonstrate a quiet voice.

Let the children eat their meal or snack. Whenever you see a child using a quiet voice or table manners, put a stamp design on his or her placemat. Be sure each child gets several designs stamped. Use the placemats at each meal or snack and vary the rubber stamp used each time. Let the children take their placemats home at the end of the week.

Hint: Use rubber stamps that reflect a theme your children are studying or an upcoming holiday.

Airplane Ride

Try this high-flying Bear Hug for a change of pace.

Materials: Cart, wagon, or cardboard box; your children's meals or snacks.

Preparation: Place the meals or snacks in the cart, wagon, or box.

Activity: Ask your children to sit down to eat. Tell them that they are going to ride on an airplane while they eat today. Pretend to be the pilot and give them instructions to prepare for takeoff such as "Sit still," "Buckle up," and "Hands in lap." Then pretend to take off.

When the plane is in the air, select two children to be the flight attendants. Have the children push the cart around and give each child his or her food. When the children are finished eating, choose two more children to collect the garbage. After the garbage is collected, pretend to land the plane and help the children "disembark" to their next destination.

Hint: If you prepare the meal or snack, serve the food on partitioned frozen-food trays.

Snowball Fun

Try this Bear Hug when you want to make meals and snacks more calm.

Materials: Small plastic containers; cotton balls; construction paper; glue; felt-tip markers.

Preparation: None.

Activity: As your children begin to eat, pass out the plastic containers. Explain to them that you will be putting cotton-ball "snowballs" into their containers when you see them using table manners or visiting quietly. Tell them that after they finish eating, they may use their snowballs to make an art project.

Then let the children eat. When you notice a child talking quietly and using table manners, drop a snowball into his or her container. If desired, mention what you noticed the child doing such as saying thank you, visiting quietly, or using a napkin. Continue while the children are eating. Be sure each child receives several snowballs.

At the end of the meal or snack, set out paper, glue, and felt-tip markers. Let the children glue their snowballs onto the construction paper to create pictures.

Surprise Egg

Use this seasonal Bear Hug to help your children remember to use quiet voices while eating.

Materials: White butcher paper; scissors; small fluffy chick for each child (purchased or made by gluing plastic moving eyes on yellow pompons or cotton balls); paper bag; tape; black felt-tip marker.

Preparation: Cut a large egg shape out of the white paper. Put the chicks in the bag. Tape the bag to the back of the egg shape. Then hang the shape on a wall near the tables used for eating.

Activity: Point out the Surprise Egg to your children. Explain that inside the egg there is a surprise getting ready to hatch. Tell the children that they can help the surprise hatch by keeping a quiet, calm atmosphere whenever they are eating. When the children are eating quietly and calmly, gently draw a short crack line on the Surprise Egg, starting at one side. Explain that when the crack goes across the whole egg, whatever is inside will be ready to come out.

Extend the line periodically throughout the eating time, whenever the noise level is appropriate. When the noise is too loud, do not draw any more. Help the children notice that the crack in the Surprise Egg grows when they are quiet and stays put when they are noisy. Then let them help one another be quiet.

When the crack goes all the way across the Surprise Egg, tell the children that the surprise is now ready to come out. Remove the bag from behind the egg. Let each child reach into the bag and pull out a baby chick.

Hint: For younger children, draw the cracked line quickly enough for the egg to hatch in one day. For older children, extend the activity over the course of a week.

The Magic Bird

*Add some suspense to your children's meals
or snacks with this Bear Hug.*

Materials: Paper or plastic grass; basket; toy animal to represent a bird; stickers or other treats, one for each child.

Preparation: Place the paper grass in the basket and arrange the bird on top.

Activity: Introduce your children to the Magic Bird sitting in the basket. Explain that the bird is magic because instead of laying eggs, like other birds, it lays special treats. But it can only lay these treats in a place that is quiet.

Place the basket with the Magic Bird near the tables where the children eat. Encourage them to maintain a calm noise level so the bird will lay a surprise. Throughout the eating time, choose children who are sitting quietly to peek in the basket to see if the noise level has been low enough for the bird to lay its surprise.

At the end of the meal or snack, secretly place the stickers under the bird. Select a child to check one last time for a surprise. When the stickers are found, pass one out to each child.

Variation: Instead of a toy bird, use a toy dinosaur, a spider, a turtle, a fish, or another animal that lays eggs.

TOTLINE® BOOKS

NEW! Busy Bees—Fall
Attention-getting activities with a fun fall agenda! Includes simple songs, rhymes, snacks, movement, art, and science projects.
WPH 2405

1•2•3 SERIES
Beginning hands-on activities—creative art, no-lose games, puppets, and more. For ages 3 to 6.

1•2•3 Art
160 pages of art activities emphasizing the creative process.
WPH 0401

1•2•3 Games
70 no-lose games to foster creativity and decision making.
WPH 0402

1•2•3 Reading & Writing
Activity ideas for developing *pre-reading* and *pre-writing* skills.
WPH 0407

1•2•3 Rhymes, Songs & Stories
Open-ended rhymes, songs, and stories to capture imaginations.
WPH 0408

1•2•3 Math
Activities galore for experiencing number concepts.
WPH 0409

1•2•3 Science
Fun, wonder-filled activities that get children excited about science.
WPH 0410

THEME-A-SAURUS®
Instant theme ideas to capture those special teaching moments.

Theme-A-Saurus
Over 50 themes from Apple to Zebras.
WPH 1001

Theme-A-Saurus II
60 themes from Ants to Zippers.
WPH 1002

Toddler Theme-A-Saurus
60 teaching themes for toddlers.
WPH 1003

Alphabet Theme-A-Saurus
26 giant letter-recognition units.
WPH 1004

Nursery Rhyme Theme-A-Saurus
Nursery rhymes with fun, related learning activities.
WPH 1005

Storytime Theme-A-Saurus
12 storytime favorites with related activities.
WPH 1006

1001 SERIES
These easy-to-use books are the ultimate resources for teachers and parents of young children.

1001 Teaching Props
These 1001 ideas make teaching easy! Also includes a handy materials index!
WPH 1501

1001 Teaching Tips
These shortcuts to success help save time and money.
WPH 1502

1001 Rhymes & Fingerplays
A complete language resource with rhymes for all occasions!
WPH 1503

NEW! Play & Learn with Magnets
Fun and inexpensive activities that explore the versatile play and learn opportunities of magnets.
WPH 2301

NEW! Play & Learn with Rubber Stamps
Around-the-curriculum fun with simple rubber stamps. Perfect for ages 3 to 8.
WPH 2302

PIGGYBACK® SONGS
New songs to the tunes of childhood favorites. No music to read. Easy! Chorded for guitar/autoharp.

Piggyback Songs
Original songs for each season.
WPH 0201

More Piggyback Songs
More seasonal songs!
WPH 0202

Piggyback Songs for Infants and Toddlers
Songs for infants and toddlers.
WPH 0203

Holiday Piggyback Songs
More than 250 original songs for 15 holidays and other celebrations.
WPH 0206

Animal Piggyback Songs
More than 200 songs about farm, zoo, and sea animals.
WPH 0207

Piggyback Songs for School
Delightful songs to use throughout the school day.
WPH 0208

Piggyback Songs to Sign
Signing phrases to use each month along with new Piggyback Songs.
WPH 0209

EXPLORING SERIES
Instill the spirit of exploration with these beginning science books that let you take activities as far as your children's interest will go.

Exploring Sand and the Desert
Set up a child-directed learning environment with hands-on activity suggestions for learning at the sand table and about the desert environment and how to preserve it.
WPH 1801

Exploring Water and the Ocean
This 96-page book is water fun at its best. An around-the-curriculum unit about water, plus an introduction to the ocean environment with an emphasis on preservation.
WPH 1802

Exploring Wood and the Forest
Set up a child-directed learning environment with activities for developing early carpentry skills and knowledge about trees and forests.
WPH 1803

SNACK SERIES
A most delicious way to combine nutrition with fun and learning!

Super Snacks
Seasonal snacks with no sugar, honey, or artificial sweeteners! Includes CACFP information.
WPH 1601

Healthy Snacks
Healthy alternatives to junk-food snacks, plus CACFP information. Low fat, sugar, and sodium!
WPH 1602

Teaching Snacks
Promotes the teaching of basic skills through the joy of cooking.
WPH 1603

Children's Books
with Related Activities and Songs

Get two books in one: a beautifully illustrated story plus related activities & songs.

NATURE SERIES
Beautiful stories that focus on changes and differences in nature.

NEW! The Bear and the Mountain
Themes: Bears, Flowers, Friendship
Experience the joy of friendship as a playful bear cub and a lonely mountain get to know each other.
PB • WPH 1905
HB • WPH 1906

Ellie the Evergreen
Themes: Fall, Winter, Self-esteem
When the trees in the park turn colors in the fall, Ellie the Evergreen feels left out, until something special happens to her too.
PB • WPH 1901
HB • WPH 1902

The Wishing Fish
Themes: Trees, North/South, Hot/Cold
Enjoy the misadventures of a palm tree and a fir tree as they get their wish to move to a different climate —thanks to the Rainbow Fish.
PB • WPH 1903
HB • WPH 1904

HUFF & PUFF SERIES
Enjoy the monthly adventures of two endearing clouds, Huff & Puff.

NEW! Huff and Puff Go to School
Themes: School, Numbers, Colors
Huff and Puff set off for school in the sky to learn and play.
PB • WPH 2009
HB • WPH 2010

Huff and Puff on Halloween
Themes: Halloween, Being Afraid
Huff and Puff turn a mischievous trick into a giant treat.
PB • WPH 2001
HB • WPH 2002

Huff and Puff on Thanksgiving
Themes: Thanksgiving, Families
Huff and Puff celebrate Thanksgiving with friends and family.
PB • WPH 2003
HB • WPH 2004

NEW! Huff and Puff's Foggy Christmas
Themes: Christmas, Fog, Curiosity
Huff and Puff almost ruin Christmas by spying on Santa.
PB • WPH 2011
HB • WPH 2012

Huff and Puff's April Showers
Themes: Rain, Flowers, Mother's Day
Huff and Puff's misfortune turns into a wonderful gift for mother.
PB • WPH 2005
HB • WPH 2006

Huff and Puff Around the World
Themes: Transportation, Foreign Lands
Huff and Puff circle the globe and explore new places.
PB • WPH 2007
HB • WPH 2008

Cut & Tell Cutouts

Enjoy instant storytime fun with these full-color, inexpensive folder stories. Each one contains a traditional nursery tale or rhyme retold by Jean Warren; beautifully illustrated, full-color cutouts ready to turn into flannelboard or magnet board manipulatives or stick puppets; songs, poems, and learning games. Each folder story is 8 pages.

NEW!

NURSERY TALES

The Gingerbread Kid
WPH 2201

Henny Penny
WPH 2202

The Three Bears
WPH 2203

The Three Billy Goats Gruff
WPH 2204

Little Red Riding Hood
WPH 2205

The Three Little Pigs
WPH 2206

NUMBER RHYMES

Hickory, Dickory Dock
WPH 2207

Humpty Dumpty
WPH 2208

1, 2, Buckle My Shoe
WPH 2209

Old Mother Hubbard
WPH 2210

Rabbit, Rabbit, Carrot Eater
WPH 2211

Twinkle, Twinkle, Little Star
WPH 2212

TWO GREAT NEWSLETTERS

from the publisher of Totline books. Perfect for parents and teachers of young children. Get FRESH IDEAS. Keep up with what's new. Keep up with what's appropriate. Help your children feel good about themselves and their ability to learn, using the hands-on approach to active learning found in these two newsletters.

Warren Publishing House, Inc.
P.O. Box 2250, Dept. Z
Everett, WA 98203

Totline®

Instant hands-on ideas for early childhood educators & parents!

This newsletter offers challenging and creative hands-on activities for ages 2 to 6. Each bimonthly issue includes • seasonal fun • learning games • open-ended art • music and movement • language activities • science fun • reproducible patterns and • reproducible parent-flyer pages. Every activity is designed to make maximum use of common, inexpensive materials.

Sample issue $2

Individual and Group Subscriptions Available

Super Snack News

Nutritious food, facts and fun!

This monthly newsletter features four pages of healthy recipes, nutrition tips, and related songs and activities for young children. Also provided are portion guidelines for the CACFP government program. Sharing *Super Snack News* is a wonderful way to help promote quality childcare. A Reproducible Subscription allows you the right to make up to 200 copies.

Sample issue $1

Individual and Reproducible Subscriptions Available